How To Cook a Peacock:

Le Viandier

by

Taillevent

Translated by
Jim Chevallier

THIRD EDITION

ISBN: 978-1-4382-1012-4

To contact the translator, e-mail: *jimchev@chezjim.com*

Published by:

Chez Jim
North Hollywood, CA

Table of Contents

NOTE: *The headings for the Viander itself are as in the original transcription. The index provides a more accurate guide to general subjects and specific ingredients.*

TAILLEVENT

Did the French king's cook have a big nose?

This is one explanation given for the nickname "Taillevent" ("Slice-wind") given to Guillaume Tirel, the fourteenth century cook who served three kings (Philip VI, Charles V and Charles VI), among other luminaries. The portrait on his tomb however does not show a pronounced proboscis. What is sure is that a cookbook credited to him was long regarded as the first professional French cookbook. The discovery of a similar work that predates his birth has not dislodged him from his place in French culinary history, and a famous restaurant in Paris still bears his name.

The work's title, *Le Viandier*, can only be translated into archaic English as "The Viander" or "The Victualler". Though in modern French *viande* means "meat", at this time it referred to any food, and so the closest modern sense of the title is, quite simply, "cookbook". Several very different versions of the book exist. This translation is of the so-called "Fifteenth Century" version, which is the least coherent and most fragmentary of the few versions known. The recipes in it range from fairly detailed explanations, complete with measurements, to cursory suggestions of how to serve the dish in question (with no real explanation of how to make it). For a modern reader, the ingredients range from the familiar — chicken, eggs, peas, etc. — to the exotic; some would say barbaric: heron, stork, swan . — and yes, peacock.

i

NOTES AND GLOSSARIES

This is a reasonably accurate, reasonably complete translation of a work that is itself incomplete and corrupt. If some passages seem redundant, illogical or confused, it's very likely that's how they were in the original French. In some cases, I have interpreted ambivalent references to give them their most likely sense; for other words, it seemed best to let the reader decide for themselves. I have sometimes either deleted a word or phrase (indicated by "…") or left it in French. Some of the words used here seem *only* to occur in this work; others may have been so garbled in transcription that no useful guess can be made as to the intended word. Some, too, are used in ways that have no relation to their meaning either in modern French or as defined in older dictionaries.

Several special classes of words exist here, which are addressed in the following mini-glossaries:

- Old French terms left untranslated (or adapted into archaic English equivalents)
- Non-standard uses of familiar French words
- Unusual ingredients

Old French terms left untranslated

Many titles of dishes have been left in French, either because they have no real equivalent in English or because any translation would be too general to be useful. These are the most common:

Brewet (*Brouet*) This word once meant 'soup' or 'broth' – as did a number of other names of dishes here. To complicate matters, the old idea of a soup was more solid than liquid. Here and in other cases, I've kept the old word in its Anglicized form.

Pastie (*Pasté*) Strictly speaking, this refers to food – usually meat in pâté – in a pastry shell, something like a meat pie or a *pâté en croûte*. The pastry itself, however, may have been too hardened to eat. Many of the recipes here really refer to the contents of the pastie – that is, effectively, to a pâté. Also, many of these are not really recipes so much as suggestions on how to accompany the dishes named.

Non-standard uses of familiar French words

Brown or simmer for *souffrire*

"Souffrire" means to suffer. However, I suspect this spelling of the word is a slight mistranscription of "sousfrire" – that is, to "under-fry". Though the *Menagier de Paris* says that a similar word means to fry in a pot rather than a frying pan, we are told at least once here to "souffrire" something in a frying pan. In context, it seems to mean to brown the food, or, when liquid is present, to simmer it (especially since the modern word for that – "mijoter" – does not appear here.)

Infuse for *deffaire*

"Deffaire" means to undo or break up. Here, though, the sense is to 'break up" in liquid – that is, to dissolve, moisten or infuse spices or other solid matter.

Restore for *reffaire*

"Reffaire" means to redo or to restore (as in restoring a house). As an old cooking term, it means to "restore" meat to a fresh, succulent state before cooking it. Some dictionaries say specifically to do this by grilling it lightly. However, several recipes refer to doing this in cold or hot water. A modern cook might do this by blanching or "brining" meat (in a sugar and salt brine). In practice, it is an excellent way to keep chicken tenders (for instance) moist when grilling them.

Sturgeon for *esturgon*

In this case, the translation is nearly direct. But neither dish under that name includes sturgeon. Were these assumed to include that fish, or are they replacements for it? Or did the word once have another meaning (so far unknown)?

Several other terms, such as "vinaigrette" and "blancmange", are also used in ways unrelated to their modern meanings.

Unusual ingredients

Verjuice

The most common definition of this is as the tart juice of a specific grape when under-ripe. But various sources suggest it was a more general term for a "green juice". Cotgrave's dictionary (1611) defines the French word as follows: "**Verjus**: m. Verjuice, especially that which is made of sowre, and unripe grapes; also, the grapes whereof it is made". Legrand d'Aussy says that it was originally the 'sweat' of sorrel, but this may just have been a method for replacing or reinforcing the grape version. "Verjuice of grain" might refer to either a verjuice made from young wheat (again per Legrand) or using the verjuice grapes themselves. Lemon juice or vinegar are two modern replacements. Though some writers discuss this ingredient as if it were specific to medieval times, in fact it was still used in the late nineteenth century, and can still be obtained from specialized sources.

Seed or **Paradise Seed**

Paradise seed, a rarer, pricier cousin to cardamom, is still used for brewing. Cardamom and pepper together are one possible replacement.

Powder (Fine Powder) and **Duke's Powder**

These are different mixtures of spices used to season dishes (like salt or pepper) after cooking. Both are made up of the same spices used in many recipes here: ginger, cinnamon, clove, etc. The proportions probably varied in different households. (The five-spice mix sold today in Chinese markets is similar, though it often includes anise.)

Almond Milk

Basically, this is obtained by grinding up almonds, mixing them with water and pressing out the resulting liquid. Different recipes exist for this. Some stores also offer a modern, more complex equivalent.

THE VIANDER

Here follows the viander to prepare all manners of victuals that Taillevent, chief cook of the king our lord, did so much to dress and to prepare gruel, roast, salt water and fresh water fish: With this, sauces, spices and other things suitable and necessary, as will be said below.

And firstly of the first chapter.

[The original includes a cursory table of contents at this point]

Here ends the table and begins the matter of this book.

To Make White Brewet Of Capons

Or poultry or veal, it is best to boil it and take the broth, once it is cooked, and to put it aside. Blanch the almonds, and crush them, and soak them in the broth of the poultry, capons or veal, and then strain the almonds through a cheesecloth, and take a reasonable quantity of powdered white ginger, and infuse with verjuice and white wine, and put a large quantity of large lumps of sugar to boil. When it is boiled, put the broth separately in a nice pot and also the meats (that is, the poultry, capon or veal), and, when serving it, put your meats in a dish with your broth.

To Make Blancmange of Fish

Of pike, perch or other fish suitable for blancmange, and scale it, and fry with oil or butter and take almonds, and mix them as above, and pea puree. Add white wine and mix, and add white ginger, and infuse with verjuice and enough sugar, and set it apart as with that for meat.

To Make White German Brewet

Take veal or poultry, and restore it, and then cut it up into pieces. Set to simmer with a nice beef broth and lard, and put in an onion finely cut. Crush almonds with the skins, and infuse with beef broth, and strain. While straining, put in poultry livers and almonds, and when the broth is strained, put it in the pot, when the meat is cooked and put a moderate amount of sugar in the pot while simmering, and the appropriate spices: that is, cinnamon,

1

ginger, assorted spices (clove and paradise seed), and saffron for color. Infuse with verjuice, white wine or red Burgundy wine, and then serve, when the time comes, in plates or bowls.

To Make Salamine

Take pike, carp or other fish of the sort, and scale it, and fry it. Crush up almonds with the skins, infuse with purée of peas, then take the same spices as for the German Brewet, and infuse with verjuice. Boil your broth, and set it apart until it is time to serve it.

To Make Brewet Georget

Take veal, poultry or rabbit, cut up in pieces and grill lightly. When it is browned, fry it in a little lard and some beef broth, and add some finely cut raw onion. Fry with the meat, and put some parsley leaves in it. Brown some bread, and, when it is browned, soak it in beef broth and put in poultry livers and strain with the meat. Beat and crush the spices which go with it (cinnamon, ginger, clove and seed), and infuse with verjuice. Add saffron for color, and put it all in a pot. When ready, serve it in dishes or bowls

To Make Fish Grané

Take pike, carp or other fish. Scale and fry the fish. Then toast bread, and soak it in purée of peas, strain it, and put in fried onion sliced large. Boil it all together, with ginger, cinnamon and various spices, infused with vinegar, and add a bit of saffron for color.

To Make Cinnamon Brewet With Meat

Take veal and poultry, and cut up into pieces. Grill them lightly. Then fry, with a little lard, and also some beef broth. Then take almonds crushed with the skins, and infuse with sufficient beef broth, and take poultry livers, and strain with the almonds. Then take some spices, that is, a very large quantity of cinnamon, ginger, clove and paradise seed, and crush up the spice and infuse with red Burgundy wine. Add a large quantity of sugar, and salt as appropriate.

For That Of Fish

Take carp, pike or another fish, and scale it, and fry it, and make the broth like that for meat, except with pea puree, and put similar spices as for meat, and sweeten as with the other, and season like the other, and boil your broth, and set your broth apart and the fish in the other.

To Make A Cretonnée Of New Peas

Or with new broad beans or whatever legume you desire: cut veal or kid up in parts and poussins, with the legume that goes with it, and then fry it with lard or other fat, with whatever broth you have available to put over it. Boil milk in a pot or frying pan, with egg yolks to thicken, and, when it is thickened, infuse with ginger. Put it in, and salt to taste.

To Make Thin (Fasting) Pottage

Take new peas or new broad beans, and similar broth as for meat. And to thicken with poached eggs, make as above but do not add ginger to this thickening. Season it as appropriate.

To Make Spanish Cretonnée

Take veal or poultry cut in pieces, and cook the meat, and fry with lard or any shortening you can find. Take almonds, and strain, and make milk of them or use milk if you have it, and take parsley and marjoram, if you have it, and throw a good deal in. Strain with the greenery, and, when the milk is boiled, you thicken as with eggs. Beat together ginger and assorted spices, and infuse with verjuice and white wine. When your soup is ready and thickened, put it in a pot. When it is time to serve, take hard-boiled eggs, and shell them and split them down the middle. Then fry them with lard. When the broth is in your dish, if you want to put your eggs on it, or browned toasts, they will look lovely there.

For Fish Cretonnée

Take carp or pike, scaled, and fry when it is in pieces, and make your broth as for that of meat, except that it is made with pea puree, and the other is made with meat broth, and all the rest is made like that for meat.

To Make Green Brewet

Take veal and poultry, cut up in pieces. Grill them lightly and fry in lard and beef broth. Take a large amount of parsley, and strain with

3

egg yolks. To thicken, add in bread soaked together with the beef broth, and for spices, beaten ginger and a little assorted spices, diluted with verjuice.

To Make Fish Brewet

Slice up eels, and scale and slice up pike. Boil in water and pea puree, and put herbs, spices and verjuice, as above, and egg yolks; and set the broth separately.

For Covered Brewet

Take veal or poultry, cut up in pieces, and simmer in a pot with lard and beef broth, and take bread soaked in beef broth, and poultry livers, and cook in a separate pot: the parsley, the costmary, marjoram, wild spinach, cooked egg yolks, and strain it all together, and take a great quantity of parsley, raw, and crush, and strain with the broth. And then boil the spices, that is cinnamon, ginger, paradise seed and clove, and infuse with verjuice, and boil it all together.

To Make Civet Of Hare

Brown a hare, veal or pig on the spit or on the grill. Cut up into pieces and put in a pot. Fry it in lard and beef broth in a pot. Take bread and livers, and strain. Fry onion in lard and throw in the pot with the meat, and add in the broth. When the bread is strained, put it all in a pot, with the following spices: cinnamon, ginger, paradise seed, clove, and nutmeg if you have it, diluted with vinegar, and put it all together.

For Lark Grané

Take larks, restore them, then brown, and put veal in the pot with them, for a better broth. Brown the bread and soak it in beef broth. Soak livers with the bread and strain. Once it has been strained, put everything together in the pot and cinnamon, ginger and assorted spices, diluted with verjuice.

For Shrimp Grané

Take shrimp, and cook them. Once they are properly cooked and salted to taste, you will shell them, and put the shells aside, and fry them, not too much, and crush the bodies of the shrimp in the mortar and almonds with the skins, and strain the almonds all together. And put cinnamon, ginger and assorted spices, and infuse with verjuice, and boil them all together, add a reasonable amount of sugar, and salt to taste. And if you do not have enough meat, take pike and put in place of the shrimp.

To Make Chaudumé

Take eels, pike browned on the grill, cut up and put in a frying pan or a pot; and, when they are browned, take some puree, set it to boil, and strain pike livers with it. Add ginger, and saffron for color, to the chaudumé, and take verjuice and wine to put with chaudumé, and boil everything together, and sprinkle with salt.

To Make Mustard Soup

For a fish day, fry eggs in oil or butter, and then use pure mustard, cinnamon, ginger, assorted spices such as cloves and seed, and sweeten moderately. Strain it all together and boil in a pot, and infuse it with verjuice. Salt to taste, and put the broth apart.

For Partridge Trimolette

Take partridge, and roast it. When it is roasted, fry it in a pot with lard and beef broth, and then fry finely chopped onion. Put with the other spices, and paradise seed, and sweeten moderately. Take browned bread and poultry livers of, if you have them, and soak in beef broth, and strain through cheesecloth and pour in the pot with the partridge. Add what is appropriate: cinnamon, ginger, assorted spices, clove, paradise seed. Infuse with verjuice. Salt to taste.

For Seyme

Put some rabbits to brown on the spit or on the grill. Cut up in pieces, and fry in a pot, with lard and beef broth to make the broth., Take bread and livers, if you have them, and soak in the beef broth. Then strain the bread and the livers, and put in the pot, Take ginger, cinnamon and assorted spices, infused with verjuice, and boil all together, and salt to taste.

For Gibelet Of River Bird

Brown the birds on the spit or on the grill. Make similar broth as for seyme, and verjuice, with the same spices.

For Larded Boil of Rabbit or Poultry

Cut up in pieces, and lard each one with a lardoon or two. Boil in a pot in of beef broth to cook it. Then take ginger, cinnamon and assorted spices, and verjuice and salt to taste.

For Brewet Rappé

Take veal, poultry, cut up in pieces, and fry in a pot with lard and beef broth. Put some bread in to soak, and strain; and put in seed ginger, with no other spices – this is enough. When the potage is ready, take verjuice of grain or gooseberries on it.

To Make Venison In Soup

Take venison cut up in nice big parts and boil them, each one with its lardoons. Boil in a pot with some beef broth, if you have it, or its own broth, and add some red Burgundy wine, the best that you can find. For spices, clove and seeds, and crush them and soak in verjuice and a little vinegar. Boil it all together, and salt to taste.

Venison Of Deer

Put in soup as for the other above.

Venison Of Wild Boar

To put in soup or pottage, boil it thus. Put in a pot and cook in wine and beef broth, and other broth. Take some browned bread and soak in a little broth. For spices, put cinnamon, paradise seed, clove, and a lot of ginger in the pot with the venison.

To Make A Sorvige Of Eels

Take scalded eels. Clean and cut up. Fry onion and parsley. Once it is cut into round sections and fried, put it in your pot. Take browned bread, and soak it in pea purée. It is best to strain it. Put in a pot, and some spices, that is ginger, cinnamon and assorted spices. Add to the pot, and saffron for color, infused with vinegar.

To Make A Mock Grenon

Take a pig buttock and cook it. When it is not too well cooked along the side, slice it up in large cubes, and take some small giblets of poultry, such as livers, gizzards, etc, and set them to cook. When they are cooked, slice up partridge, and fry them in its broth. Take white bread and soak it in the broth in which the pig was cooked if you have no beef broth and also mix in egg yolks with your bread. Add some ginger and a little saffron, some white wine and verjuice, and let the color soak in. After straining it through cheesecloth, boil it all together, without leaving it too long on the fire. Then put the broth in a pot, and season with salt.

To Make Cold Sage

Take poussins split along the back, and giblets (such as gizzards and livers). Slice up the giblets. When the poussins are cooked, and prepared, slice them lengthwise, and serve them in dishes or bowls, with the appropriate sauce, such as green sauce - it makes no difference which as long as there is sage. When serving, put very well cooked eggs on the plates in halves.

To Make Red [Dish]

Take poussins and veal, and boil and, once they are cooked, fry them in lard; take peeled almonds, crushed up and ground fine, and soak them in the poultry broth. Then take a moderate amount of rose water, and strain with the almonds and the broth, and put in a pot, with some verjuice, and just a little white wine, and take some powdered rice and infuse with rose water, so that, when your soup is on the fire and it boils, it thickens. Put in a large amount of sugar. And to give a red color, take orchanet [EDITOR'S WARNING: *Several modern herbals warn AGAINST taking this herb, also known as alkanets, internally*], and heat in lard, the best lard you can find, and filter into the pot to give it color. When the meat is served in dishes, put the broth over it and gilded garlic bulbs, two or three with each dish, or some white sugared almonds, if you have them.

To Make A Violet [Dish]

Take veal and whole poussins, and cook them. Simmer them in a pot after in the broth of your veal and of your poussins. Take peeled almonds, and crush them and strain them. Once they are strained, put them in a pot to boil, and add a generous, but reasonable, amount of sugar. Then take white wine and verjuice, and mix in beaten rice flour and some broth, and color it, and some *toressot* of violet to give color to the soup, and throw it in when you boil it. Salt to taste. Serve it with the broth poured over it and on that sugared almonds.

For Jelly

Take leg of lamb or foot of veal, whichever you can find, and boil in white wine with the appropriate meat. After the leg of lamb or foot of veal is about half cooked, take pork cut into pieces, and halved poussins, well cleaned, and washed, and young rabbits, if you can find them. Then take ginger and seed, a little mastic, and a lot of saffron, and a moderate amount of vinegar. And when the meat is cooked, take the broth, and put in a pot on the coal fire. If the jelly is too fatty, take eggs whites and put with the broth, when it starts to boil; and, when it boils, have a cloth right at hand to strain it with; while it is straining, put the meat in dishes, that is, the pork, the young rabbit and poultry, and then when the meat is in dishes, put in a cellar, and pour the broth on the meat in each dish.

To Make Vinaigrette

Take small pieces of pig spleen browned on the spit or on the grill, and cut up in small pieces. Put in a pot, and take some finely chopped onion, and cook. Once it is cooked, put with the meat. Add cinnamon and ginger and some assorted spices, and a bit of saffron for color. Infuse the spices with a little vinegar. Boil it all together, and salt just enough.

Bousac

For bousac, a hare is to be restored, parboiled and cut up in pieces, then put in a pot to brown, with beef broth in the pot to brown it. Brown bread. Once it is browned, soak it with poultry livers. Then strain it. Add cinnamon, ginger and assorted spices (that is, clove and seed) to the bread, and infuse the spices with vinegar. Boil it all together with verjuice and good red Burgundy wine.

Geese Treason-Style

To make geese treason-style, brown the geese on the spit. When they are browned, fry them in a pot. Put in lard and beef broth. Take cinnamon, seed and clove, and crush, if the spices are not well beaten. Put the spices in the pot with it to brown, with a moderate amount of sugar. Take a little bread and poultry livers, and soak in broth beef, and a moderate amount of mustard. Strain and put with the pot, and boil it all together. Salt to taste.

Rice

For rice, take some rice, wash it and take cow's milk of cow or milk of peeled almonds. Boil the cow's milk. When it is cooked, put a little saffron for color, and salt to taste.

Fish Arbalesty

For fish arbalesty, cook tripe of pike and carp, then leave to cool. Take a carp or two and pike, and prepare it, removing the bones as best you can. When the fish is scaled, slice into large chunks, and the tripe as well, and fry them, and the tripe of fish, that is the livers, the crops of pike and their broth. Brown bread very well without burning it and soak in pea purée and red Burgundy wine, the best you can find. Take cinnamon, ginger, assorted spices, and a large amount of clove. Strain the bread and the spices together, and infuse with vinegar. Then boil. When it is boiled, put the broth in a pot, and put the fried fish in the pot, and salt it well.

Galantine

For pike and eels in galantine, take pike and prepare them, and slice them up. Scald the eels, then slice them up, remove their bones, and tie them all around. Once they are chopped up fine, cook in a pot or frying pan, in wine. While cooking, add a little vinegar. When the eel is on the point of being cooked, add the cut up pike. When it is cooked, take the broth and put in an earthen pot or another of wood, so long as it does not smell of brass. Take bread, slice it into round slices, brown without burning, and soak in the broth that you will have filtered from the fish, then strain. When it is strained, take spices, that is cinnamon, ginger, paradise seed, clove and beaten galanga, and also any other spices, and, while boiling, put the spices in all together with the broth, and boil as long as you can without burning. Add salt as appropriate. When they are boiled, put in a wooden or earthen vessel to cool. Strain again one time, and add sugar. When it is strained, put the pike and eel in by sections, and add the liquid.

Larded Milk

To make larded milk, boil milk on the fire. Take some eggs and beat very well. Put in some white ginger, and beat with your eggs, with a little saffron for color. Take some fatty lard, slice it up finely, then cook it in a pot or frying pan. Strain it until there is no liquid left and pour it in all together with the eggs and the milk. Add salt. When you have put it all together and it is boiled, put it in a tablecloth or a hand towel, and tie it up. Press it as well as you can. When it has been pressed a whole night, the following day, slice it into thin slices. When it is sliced up, fry it in lard or pork fat.

To Make A Morterel

It is best to use pheasant, or partridge, or capon meat, or tripe of kid and thighs of kid and some of all these four things. Boil, and take their broth. Chop up the meat as finely as you can. Put in a pot and boil. When it is on the point of being cooked, take bread crumbs to put with the broth. Mix just a little cheese, good and fine, and chop it as fine as you can. Put in the pot. Take spices, beaten white ginger, moistened with just a little verjuice. Mix in eggs to thicken your morterel. When everything is cooked, take it off the fire.

Poussin Sabourot

To make sabourot of poussins, take poussins or poultry, and cut up into small pieces. Brown in a frying pan with lard. Brown a little onion. Soak the poultry in beef broth, with a little bread to thicken, and strain. Put in some beaten white ginger and a little verjuice, and salt to taste.

Quail Brewet

For quail brewet, take prepared capons or large poultry, and boil in a pot. When the meat is cooked, season with a little cooked lard. Add saffron. Take out the meat and mix in egg yolks. Strain through a cloth or beat very well. Thicken the broth with it, and add some verjuice while thickening, and beaten white ginger, and add some parsley leaves, and put it all in. When it is ready, put the meat in dishes and, when serving, some broth.

For Fried Cream

Take cream and boil and then white bread broken into small crumbs and put it in the cream, or a large quantity of crumbled wafers and put with the cream. Take egg yolks stirred in with the milk and cream, and boil it all together. Add a large quantity of sugar, and salt to taste.

For Haricoq

To make haricoq, take sheep bellies and brown them on the grill. When they are browned, cut up them into pieces, and put in a pot. Take peeled onions, and chop them up fine. Put in the pot with the meat. Take white ginger, cinnamon and assorted spices, that is, clove and seed. Moisten with verjuice and add to the pot. Salt to taste.

Wild Boar Head Cheese

To make head cheese of wild boar, take its head, when taken in heat, and split it and clean it, and boil in wine and vinegar. When it is as if rotted from cooking, then take it from the fire. Put on a table. Remove all meat from the bones. Put the skin aside, and brown the meat. Add spices to the meat: beaten cinnamon, ginger, assorted spices in large quantity, and well beaten clove and nutmeg. Put it all together. Then take the skin and put the meat back in it. Put in a piece of cloth like a headscarf. Press it between two dishes, with stones on it to press well. Leave as long as it is cold.

Lamb Shoulder

To stuff lamb shoulder, roast the shoulder on the spit. Do not cook it too much. Take it off the spit. Remove all the skin. Chop it up as finely as possible with cooked lard and a pig's liver, and a great deal of parsley, hyssop, pennyroyal and raw marjoram. Chop all this up with the shoulder and eight egg yolks for the stuffing. Some like to add ginger, sugar and salt. You must keep the shoulder bone stripped of meat, well and whole. Then have a veal or sheep membrane, the thinnest that you can find. Stretch it out on a plank very neatly. Put half of the stuffing on the veal or sheep membrane, and then take the bone of the shoulder and knock on it until as it enters in. After, take the extra stuffing and make as for the shoulder. Then put them on the outside of the membrane on top of the other, with two or three small wooden skewers to hold them. Then put it on the grill over a low fire, for a long while. Once this is done, gild with egg yolk on one side and with a feather on the other. When it is done, put in a dish and serve last.

For Moteaulx

[Possibly meaning "clumps" or "clods"]
To make the *moteaulx* stuffing, take poultry liver or lard, all cooked together, parsley, hyssop and raw marjoram, if you have it. Cook it all together with meat broth. When they are cooked, filter until no more liquid is left. Chop up fine and add some ginger and egg yolks. Then take a veal or kid membrane, and put the stuffing in it. Make it about half a foot long and as round as a full fist. Wrap in the membrane and put on the grill. Gild with egg yolks with the shoulder, if there is a shoulder, because this is [served as part of] a whole service.

Stuffed Poussins

To make stuffed poussins, it is advisable to scald them…, without cutting off their feet, wings or neck. Once they have been scalded, split them at the shoulders. Take everything inside, bone and meat, leaving only skin, except the head and the legs, all the way to the knee. Then take the chicken meat, a pig or poultry liver, lard, a great deal of parsley, hyssop, pennyroyal and basil, and cook it all together. Strain until there is no liquid left. After, chop it up as finely as you can. Put in a little ginger and a little saffron. Then put the stuffing back in the skin of the chicken, a needle across the opening, and do not fill it too much lest it burst. Because it is best to put it in boiling water, just a little bit, so that it solidifies. Then spit it through the bottom to the head on a small spit. Once it is crisp, gild it with egg yolks while turning, being careful not to burn it. When serving, sweeten the poussins.

To Make Sturgeon

Take tench and eels, and boil in pure white wine. Once they are well cooked, remove all the bones from the flesh of the fish. Take saffron for color, ginger and assorted spices. Put with the meat. Take the fish's skin and cover all the flesh with it. Put it in a straining cloth.

Press it in a mortar. Then slice it into fine slices, and serve it with parsley and vinegar.

Meat Sturgeon

To make a meat sturgeon, take a veal's head and feet. Scald and pluck and clean very well. After cook in wine. Add strong vinegar. This done, take off the skin of the head and the feet of veal, and salt it. Then take the veal sliced into thin slices, and rewrap it in the skin of the veal head. Then press the sturgeon and cut into beautiful thin slices with parsley and vinegar.

To Make Pheasant And Peacocks In Full Display

To make pheasant and peacocks in full display, lard and put on the spit. When they are half cooked, lard with clove, and for two servings. an ounce of powder of assorted spices, seed, clove, long pepper, and nutmeg and two ounces of true cinnamon beaten to powder. Then take one pint of rose water and one pint of vinegar and put under the roast. Stir all the spices together, and strain through a cloth. Put a quarter pound of sugar in the sauce. Then take half a pound of true cinnamon, and a handful of onion. Preserve in sugar and other household spices. When the roast is taken off the spit, put in dishes, lard with the preserved true cinnamon. Put some broth under it without touching the preserves. This sauce is good on all roasts.

To Make Fayenne

Take a pig and cook in pure wine as for jelly. Sprinkle it with the same spices as for jelly. Boil pig and poultry livers. Take a pound of almonds, and also a pound of egg yolks, and also the livers and almonds, and strain it all together through a cloth. Put, for six servings, a pound of sugar, and put in your meat, no more or less than you want for the brewet, with the jelly on it. Boil your broth, put it on the meat and cool in a spout or elsewhere.

For Cele Preserve For Four

Take two pounds of almonds, and crush them all together, whole. Take capon or poultry broth. Strain the almonds. Crush the shrimp shells like the almonds and strain with your broth through the cloth. On fish days, strain, and mix them up with a quarter pound of true cinnamon and two ounces of ginger, and add a pint of verjuice and a half pound of sugar.

To Make A Potful

of beef tongue and cow teat, cook them, and take the broth in which they are cooked. Cut up the tongues and teat into small pieces like beans. Fry in lard. Chop up onion, then brown. Take powdered ginger soaked in verjuice, and a little soaked bread. Add a little saffron for color.

For Fish Fraze

Take pike heads and roast them on the grill. Take the fish maws and livers, and chop into small cubes. Fry with butter or oil. Take the pike eggs, and strain through a cloth. Add in sugar and ginger. Put, while frying, with the maws and livers. Gild the heads on the grill. When serving at the table, put duke's powder on it.

Holy Water

To make holy water on pike, scald it and then fry it, and after put it in a dish. Take half a glass of rose water and as much verjuice, a little ginger and a moderate amount of marjoram, and the pike's liver, and boil it all together. Then strain through a cloth, and put about an eight of a pound of sugar per dish. Then put the pike on coals to stew.

For Steamed Poussins

[or] for stuffed steamed hens, take a new pot, and put them in once they are stuffed. Cover so that no steam gets out. Once they are cooked, take a pint of vinegar, an ounce of assorted spices, and put it all in the pot with a quarter pound of duke's powder. When they are well cooked, put in dishes. If you see that there is too much fat, remove it.

Almond Irson

To make almond irson for four, crush approximately four pounds of almonds in a mortar, and strain them through a cloth with a little warm water. When the almonds are thick, add a quarter pound of sugar, and boil it all in a frying pan. When it is boiled, put in a straining cloth or on a new cloth and let it cool. Put in dishes as for a bar of butter. Then take the best-looking almonds and split in half, and split each half in three parts lengthwise, and yellow the half with saffron. Then place them in nice rows along the length. Take milk, as much as suits you, and put it in barely touching the almonds.

Eggs Roasted On The Spit

To roast stuffed eggs on the spit, make a small hole in the end of each egg, and take out what is inside. Then take sage, marjoram, pennyroyal, mint and all other good herbs, and chop them up finely. Fry in butter, and the eggs, and put on a plank and chop them up finely. Add in ginger, saffron and sugar. Then put the stuffing in the egg shells. Take small, very fine skewers. Put a dozen eggs on each skewer, and set on the grill over a low fire.

Meat Vintage

For a half dozen vintages of meal, take veal or pork, and boil in a pot with herbs and lard. Put eggs in a pot separately and when the meat is half cooked, chop it up small and put in a half dozen eggs with the meat and one dozen *crus* [*literally, "wine growths" – meaning grapes, bunches of grapes or wine?*]. Take a half ounce of true cinnamon, a quarter ounce of assorted spices and add a little saffron. Take sheep stomach and pack the stuffing in it as for an andouille. Put three egg yolks studded with clove. When serving, put some duke's powder on it.

Fried Fresh Butter

To make fresh butter in a frying pan, take stale white bread, and crush up the crumbs finely. Take two ounces of starch and two ounces sugar, together with the butter, and soak the dough in eggs and sugar, without any liquid. Then make it as fine as a sheet of paper, and sprinkle the dough with egg yolks. Then wrap the bar of butter in it, and fry in the frying pan with other beef [sic]. After put in dishes and serve.

Coulis

To make coulis, take a capon and boil until well cooked. Take the white of the capon and other meat from the capon, crush it up in the mortar, and, when it is well crushed, strain through a cloth. Soak in the capon broth. Afterwards, boil in a small pot, and, when it is cooked, salt moderately, but not too much. Do not add verjuice, vinegar, or anything else.

To Make Coulis

To make another coulis for the sick, take a poussin or two, and start in the same way as the capon above, but, when crushing, add a dozen almonds to make it more substantial.

Fish Coulis

To make another fish coulis, take a perch and cook it in water. Once it is cooked, skinned, and boned, after grind it, and, in grinding it, mix in a dozen blanched almonds, soaked in purée of peas. After make like that of meat, and salt to taste without anything else in it, if the physician does not order that sugar be put in it.

Another Coulis

Take pike cooked and soaked. Make like that of perch.

Blanched Barley

To make blanched barley, beat the barley and grind it up in a mortar. After it is well cleaned, rinse and boil it very well, like wheat to make fromenty. Once it is cooked, crush it in the mortar, and then soak in almond milk. Then boil in a nice large pot and, if the sick person wants sugar in it, put some in. It can be salted or not. And if you want to make blanched whole barley, without crushing it, put some thick almond milk, and put the whole barley in it.

For Potted Pastie

Take veal or beef buttock, and chop it up finely, with fat as for a potted pastie, and finely chopped onion. To bind it, put in assorted spices, ginger, cinnamon, saffron and some verjuice.

Gallimaufrey

For gallimaufrey, roast poultry or capons, and cut into pieces. After fry with lard or goose lard. When they are fried, put in wine and verjuice. For spices, put some ginger powder and, to thicken, cameline, and a moderate amount of salt.

Fricassees

For fricassees, take raw poultry, cut up into pieces and fry in lard. While frying, put finely chopped onion and afterwards beef broth, and for spices, ginger powder soaked in verjuice; and boil it all together.

Beef Pastie

Chop meat quite small and put in in winter style. Add cheese and ginger and saffron.

Pastie With Warm Sauce

From the heart of the loin, cut into thin tender slices and chop fat over them. To make the sauce, toast black bread well, and after soak in verjuice and vinegar and strain through a cloth. The appropriate spices are: ginger, clove, long pepper, paradise seed, nutmeg, in equal parts, except the clove should dominate the other spices. Boil the sauce in an iron frying pan and, when the pastie is cooked, put the fat in the pastie. This done, add the sauce, and boil with the sauce in the oven.

Veal Pastie

Take veal and beef fat, and chop it quite small all together. The appropriate spices are ginger, true cinnamon; and, in winter style, put in fine cheese.

Pastie Of Capons

For pastie of capons, cover with lard. For spices, add some ginger, assorted spices and saffron.

Pastie Of Halebran Capons

[Probably meaning very young castrated ducks, or possibly cocks.]
Put the capons in pastie. After, remove all the meat of the capons, and beef fat, and chop all together and the said pastie, beef marrow, the hard boiled egg yolks studded with clove. For spices, put in a little ginger, true cinnamon, saffron and sweeten. Cook the said

17

spices in powder to cook as said above, with a moderate amount of sugar.

Pastie Of Capons

Put in this pastie finely chopped lard. For spices, put in ginger, assorted spices and saffron.

Chicken Pastie With Sauce Robert

Take verjuice and egg yolks, and beat all together, with fine powder. When the pastie is cooked, put it all together. It is best that the poultry be cut up.

Pigeon Pastie

Put on this pastie finely chopped lard. For spices, some ginger.

For Ringdove [Pastie]

Take warm sauce as for beef and similar spices, except it goes well with onion fried in lard.

Mutton Pastie With Welsh Onion

Chop the pastie up fine in mutton fat, with assorted spices added.

Blackbird Pastie

Take some fine cheese and put in the birds, and beef marrow, and lard finely chopped, and ginger.

Sparrow Pastie

Take beef or veal, and the fat of chopped veal, and fine cheese, assorted spices and saffron.

Wild Duck Pastie

Take some lard and, for spices, clove and ginger.

Kid Pastie

Parboil the kid and after cut up in pieces. Add lard chopped fine, and for spices, cinnamon and saffron.

Gosling Pastie

Cut the gosling up, and take, in season, new beans and parboil them. And put them in the pastie, and chopped lard. For spices, assorted spices and saffron.

Partridge Pastie

Put finely chopped lard on the partridge. For spices, ginger and clove powder.

Rabbit Pastie

Cut old ones into pieces and use the young ones whole. Sprinkle with finely chopped lard. For spices, clove, ginger, seed and pepper.

Hare Pastie

Take a large hare cut up in pieces, or the smaller one whole. Sprinkle with finely chopped lard. Add assorted spices.

Stag Pastie

Boil it and lard it and after make into pastie. Add ginger and a little pepper.

Wild Boar Pastie

Take tenderloin of wild boar, and parboil it. After, slice it into fine slices, and add assorted spices.

Lorais Pastie

[NOTE: *This is particularly incoherent in the original; the following is very much a "best guess".*]
Take white capon meat finely chopped, or a sufficient quantity of spears [*slices?*] of fish, Add spices such as sugar and true cinnamon. It is best that these be small, well made pasties, pressed between three fingers, raised up high and, when they are made, it is best to fry them in a frying pan with lard. For fish, fry it all in butter, and roll this in butter, sugar and egg and cover this base as with small pasties, and it goes well with lettuce [*this apparently refers to a pastry*], like those which are made double.

Marrow Pastie

Take marrow, without anything else, with spices and sugar mixed together. Parboil the marrow; and crush up like a ball and push between three fingers into a small pastie, raised up high and well made, and fry in lard.

Mullet Pastie

Put in the belly of a mullet verjuice of grain, fine powder and saffron.

Bream Pastie

Put fine powder and saffron on it.

Trout Pastie

Put saffron and fine powder on it.

Eel Pastie

Take saffron, fine powder and verjuice in making it, and some gooseberries.

Conger Eel Pastie

Slice up sea congers. Put in assorted spices, ginger and saffron.

Turbot Pastie

Only add white ginger.

Red Mullet Pastie

Add fine powder.

Goatfish Pastie

Only add white ginger.

Shad Pastie

With white ginger and assorted spices.

Salmon Pastie

With white ginger.

Lamprey Pastie

Only add salt. Make the sauce separately, and quite black. Take from the spice cabinet lamprey powder. Burn a piece of bread quite black and soak the burned bread in verjuice and vinegar. Strain through cloth and add the powder. After boil it, and put the sauce in a small clean pot. Once the pastrie is cooked add the sauce. After put in the oven briefly, to boil the sauce with the lamprey.

Cow Pastie

Take cheese cut in strips and a large amount of sugar, true cinnamon and a bit of assorted spice. Fry onion in butter. Once the pastie is high and raised, and rounded, gild it well, then put it in the oven.

Leg Of Lamb Pastie

Take leg of lamb and lard well with clove. Put thin slices of lard on and under it. Make the crust strong and thick, so that the contents do not leak out.

Common Tart

For common covered tarts [i.e., pies], crush up cheese, and pat it, cut fine cheese into strips and mix with eggs. Otherwise make as for uncovered tarts.

Two-Faced Tart

For two-faced tart, fine cheese and many egg yolks and sugar.

Dolphins

Lily flowers, star with fried cream, a lot of sugar and egg yolks.

Make Oblongs

Make as for a stuffed bar of fried cream, if you have some. If you cannot find cream, use fine cheese and put in nice hunks of it, and sugar.

Jacobine Tart

Covered Jacobine tart, with oranges on it, is of good fine cheese cut in thin slices, and good cream, with egg yolks mixed into it. Cut eel into sections and boil it. Seat well in the tart, before adding the cheese and the cream, with a great quantity of sugar.

Bourbonnaise Tart

For Bourbonnaise tart, use fine cheese, crushed, soaked in cream, and enough egg yolks. Knead the crust well with eggs, and cover the whole top with orange.

Covered Tart

For covered tart, soak the crust in eggs and butter. Soak the stuffing in two eggs and some water in each tart and no more. Soak butter in cheese crushed in a mortar.

Talmouse

Cut fine cheese in square pieces as small as beans. Soak the cheese well in eggs and mix all together. Soak the crust in eggs and butter.

Two Faced Tart

Two faced tart is made of fine cheese cut into cubes, well soaked in egg yolks. After take a pastry crust cooked in the oven. Once it is a little cooked, set it to cool, and cover the crust with wafers, so that nothing of it shows. Put cheese soaked in egg yolks on the wafers on the crust, layered on the wafers as thick as a finger, then cook in the oven as said. When it is cooked, take it out and let it cool. After put a large quantity of sugar on it, then [take] the crust on which it is cooked, and put on the tart, turned over on the wafers with the first layer of cheese on them, like the other side, of the thickness of a finger. When ready to dine, put in the oven, and cook like the other side. When it is cooked, take it out, turn it in a dish, and take off the crust where cooked.

Jacobine Tart

Stuff with fine cheese crushed up well, and stuffed in two fingers deep. Put in handfuls of sliced eels. The slices should be less than two fingers high. Fry them in butter, and cook them, but not too much, then put in the tart and layer over the top. For each tart, put eight or ten slices on end, and stuff it well so that the cheese comes through the slices of eel when it boils. This is how it should be made.

Apple Tart

Cut up apples into pieces, and put in figs. Clean grapes well, and put in with the apples and the figs, and mix well together. Add onion fried with butter or oil, and wine. Crush up part of the apples and soak in wine. Mix in with the other apples, crushed up, put with the surplus and add the saffron, a bit of assorted spices, true cinnamon and white ginger, anis and pygurlac [*probably a misstranscription of* pignolat, *that is candied pine nut; candied ginger might be used instead*], if you have any. Make two big pastry undercrusts. Put all the fillings together, well mixed by hand, on the thick paste of apples and other fillings. After put the top on it and cover it tightly, then gild it with saffron, put in the oven, and cook.

Raw Pear Pastie

Set on end in the pastry, and fill the hollow with the sugar, for three large pears about a quarter pound of sugar. Cover well, and gild with eggs or saffron, and put in the oven.

Bourbonnaise Tart

Crush up fine cheese, soak with cream, and enough egg yolks. Knead the crust well with eggs. Cover it with a top, and put orange all over it.

Darioles Of Cream

Crush up almonds, but do not strain them. Fry the cream well in butter. Sweeten well. [*Darioles were small pastries, so all this presumably is the filling.*]

Cameline

To make a quart of cameline, brown bread in front of a good red fire, without burning it. Then soak it in very pure red Burgundy wine in a new pot, or a dish. Once it is soaked, strain through a cloth with red Burgundy wine. Then take a pint of vinegar and a quarter pound of true cinnamon, an ounce of ginger and a quarter of an ounce of assorted spices, and salt it well. Strain the bread and spices through the cloth, and put in a nice pot.

My Lady's Sauce

To make my lady's sauce, roast a goose. Put a frying pan under it. Take the liver of the goose or other poultry, and roast on the grill. Then when it is cooked, brown one toast of bread, and soak the liver and the bread in a little broth. Strain very well through a cloth. Put in the frying pan under the goose and let it boil. Boil a dozen eggs, then take the yolks and chop them up finely. When the goose is cooked, put them over it with the sauce. If you would like it to have the taste of milk, throw in a drop or two, while boiling.

To Make Poitevin Sauce

With capons or poultry, roast them well on the spit. Take their livers, and a little browned bread and very little broth, and crush up spices in a mortar - cinnamon, ginger, assorted spices - and soak in verjuice and wine. Bring to a boil, and put in the poultry.

Jance

To make jance, peel almonds and crush in a mortar. Then strain with verjuice and white wine. Take an ounce of ginger for one pint, and strain and strain again through a cloth. Boil in a frying pan. Be sure not to put it in a pot, because it will smell of brass. And do not boil it in an iron frying pan, because it will blacken.

Garlic Sauce With Milk

To make garlic sauce with milk, brown one toast of bread on the fire. Soak it in milk. Take a half dozen cloves of garlic, and crush them up in a bowl, or with the mortar, and strain them through a cloth. Add in half an ounce of ginger, and boil in a frying pan. This sauce is good on goose or other roasts.

Red Garlic Sauce

To make red garlic sauce for a roast or boiled meat, take poultry livers. Toast a bit of bread on the fire. Soak it with the livers in a little broth. Take an ounce of true cinnamon, a half ounce of ginger, a quarter of an ounce of assorted spices. Peel half a dozen garlic cloves and strain through a cloth with red wine and vinegar. Boil in a frying pan, and then put in a nice pot.

Garlic Sauce With Mustard

To make garlic sauce with mustard, take half a dozen garlic cloves, or more if you wish, and peel, and strain through a cloth with the mustard, and a half ounce of ginger. Soak it only in verjuice. When you boil it, add butter. This sauce is good on fried whiting and other fish.

Small Wine Sauce

To make small wine sauce, soak white bread crumbs in warm white wine. Once the bread is soaked, strain through a cloth with very pure verjuice. For one pint, put in an ounce of ginger, and then skim any solid matter from the verjuice and mix it in boiling water. Leave it only a little. Filter the water, and pour the grain in the sauce.

Dodine

To make milk dodines for any river bird, take some milk and put in an iron frying pan to receive the fat of the birds. Take half an ounce of ginger for two dishes. Strain it through cloth with two or three egg yolks, and boil it all with milk. Sugar to taste. When the birds are cooked, put the dodine on them.

Dodine Of Verjuice

For another dodine of verjuice to put on river birds, capons, or other roast fowl, put verjuice on the roast in an iron frying pan. Then take hard-boiled egg yolks and a half dozen pounds of poultry, and let livers roast a little on the grill. Then strain them through the cloth with very pure verjuice. Put in a little ginger and parsley leaves, and boil everything together. Put on the roast, and some browned toasts of bread under the roast, and also in other dodines.

Jean's Must

To make Jeans' must, roast fatty capons on the spit. For four servings, put a quart of milk, and boil under the capons. Then take marjoram, a little parsley, hyssop and other good herbs. Take an ounce of ginger, and add a little saffron. Soak it in milk. Chop the herbs up, and boil together. Add half a pound of sugar. When the sauce seems thick enough, take out the capons and put in a dish, with toasts under them and pour the sauce on them.

Saupiquet

[The name suggests a tart or spicy sauce]

To make saupiquet sauce on rabbit or another roast, brown bread as for cameline, and put it to soak in broth. Melt some lard in a frying pan and chop an onion up small, and fry it. For four servings, take two ounces of true cinnamon, half an ounce of ginger and a quarter of an ounce of assorted spices. Take red wine and vinegar. Strain the bread and all the spices together. Boil in a frying pan or a pot, and then put over the roast.

Chaudumé

To make chaudumé, take pike, and scald it, and put into pieces or brown whole on the grill. Brown bread, and soak in purée of peas. Then when the bread is soaked, take verjuice and white wine, and some puree, and strain it all together with your bread. Once it has been strained, for four servings, soak an ounce of ginger in the broth, with a little saffron. Put the fish with the broth, and some fresh or salted butter.

Shad Sauce

To make sauce with shad, roast the shad in a broken dish or on the spit. Take for one shad, half an ounce of ginger and a pint of verjuice. Once the shad is half cooked, put the verjuice on the shad, and take a handful of parsley and any good herbs, and put in the sauce.

Another Shad Sauce

For another sauce with shad, take some vinegar and wine, one with the other, and take an ounce of true cinnamon, half an ounce of ginger, a bit of assorted spices, and strain it all together through a cloth, and boil, and put on the shad, either in the oven or roasted on the spit.

Sauce With Must

To make sauce with must, remove grapes from the bunch and crush up in a frying pan, and boil on fire seven or eight minutes. Put in a very little red Burgundy wine, with enough grapes, and strain it all through cloth. For four servings, take two ounces of true cinnamon, two ounces of sugar, a half ounce of ginger, and strain it all through the cloth, except the sugar. This sauce is good on larks, capons or other roast, on fried eggs, fish and all other fried things. If you lack grapes, use mulberries.

White Beets

To make white beets, boil in water, then put on a plank, and chop up fine. Squeeze them strongly between your hands, and then crush up in a mortar, and after bind with the broth of beef or another meat, or, if you do not have the broth, split lard into thin slices and fry, then bind with lard and warm water. On fish days, use butter and purée of peas.

Milled Beans

To make milled beans, put the beans to soak in the evening. Remove the black ones, and boil in river or fountain water. When they are half cooked, purée them and bind with broth, and put in lard to give them taste. When they are done cooking, put in a frying pan to cool, then strain them through a cloth. After, boil them again in a pot and strain together in the same way.

Leeks

To make leeks, take the white of the leeks and chop them up well. Wash and parboil them. When they are parboiled, purée them and put cold water on them. Squeeze out between your hands, and after put them on a plank. Chop them up, then crush them in a mortar. Once this is done, bind with beef broth. On fast days, use purée of pea and butter, and almond milk if you like.

Onion Soup

To make onion soup, peel onions and chop finely or into round slices. Brown in butter for a long while. Add a little water to keep it from burning. Mix with purée of peas or water, and add some verjuice and parsley.

Heads Of Cabbage

To make heads of cabbage, take off the top leaves, and cut into four quarters. Wash and parboil approximately a half hour. Filter out the liquid, and put some cold water over them, and squeeze them between your hands. After chop up and mix with broth of beef or another meat. On fast days, use purée of peas with butter and oil.

Gourds

For gourds, peel them and cut into round slices. Remove the seeds, if there are any. Parboil in a frying pan, then purée, and add some cold water on them. Squeeze and chop up finely. Then mix with broth of beef or other meat. Put in some cow's milk. Soak in half a dozen egg yolks. Strain the broth through a cloth with the milk. For fast days, use purée of peas or butter and almond milk.

To De-salt Soups

To de-salt soups without putting in or taking out anything, take a white cloth moistened with cold water, and put on your pot, and turn it to one side and another, and, while doing this, take your pot off the fire.

To Remove The Burnt Taste From All Soups

First empty your pot into another pot, then put in your pot a little raw baker's yeast, wrapped in a white cloth and only leave it a little.

Boiled Large Meat Like Beef, Sheep, Pig

Cook in water and salt. If it is fresh, add parsley, sage, hyssop. Eaten with green or white garlic with verjuice, salted, with mustard.

Sheep Bristle

Cut up sheep bristle into pieces. Fry everything raw in lard with finely chopped onion. Once it is well cooked, put in beef broth, wine, verjuice, sage, mastic and hyssop, and a little saffron. Boil all together.

Larded Boiled Meat

Take your venison and lard it. Cook with only mastic and saffron. Then parboil fresh venison of stag. Lard the length of the meat, then cook in a great deal of water and salt with a lot of legumes. Eat parboiled in pastry, larded, with fine powder.

Wild Kid

Prepare and eat as fresh stag.

Fresh Wild Boar

Cook fresh wild boar in water and wine, with cameline.

Capon And Veal With Herbs

For capon and veal with herbs, cook in water and salt, and add lard for flavor, with parsley, sage and hyssop.

Civet Of Singed Veal

For civet of singed veal, cook on the spit and on the grill without letting it cook entirely. Fry in lard with some onions. Then take singed bread soaked in wine and pea purée. Boil your meat. Grate ginger, cinnamon, seed, clove, and saffron for color. Add some verjuice and vinegar, and a good deal of spice.

THICK SOUPS

Pork Chaudin

Cook it in water and salt, then cut up into pieces. Brown them in lard. Take ginger, long pepper, saffron, grilled bread soaked in beef broth (since the pig's broth smells of dung) and cow's milk and strain through cloth. Take verjuice, vinegar, and cook a little in water. Put in your soup just before serving it. Add egg yolks, and boil it all together.

Cretonnée Of Peas

For cretonnée of new peas, cook the peas until they are soft, then purée, and fry in lard. Then take cow's milk, and boil briefly. Soak white bread in milk, then grate ginger and saffron. Mix in your milk. Boil. Take poussins cooked in water and cut up into parts. Fry in lard. Boil, pull back from the fire, add a large quantity of eggs.

New Bean Cretonnée

As for peas.

Cretonnée Of Poultry

For cretonnée of poultry, cook in wine and water. Cut up into parts. Fry in lard. Soak a little bread in beef broth. Strain it, and boil with your meat. Powder ginger and cumin. Infuse with wine and verjuice. Take a large quantity of egg yolks and dribble into your pot. Pull back from the fire, and watch that it does not turn.

Almond Cretonnée

For almond cretonnée, cook poultry well in water. Cut up into parts. Fry in lard. Take almonds infused with broth, and boil on your meat. Grate ginger and cumin, infuse with wine and verjuice. Always let thicken on its own, without adding anything but a little white bread.

Grané Of Small Birds

For grané of whatever assorted small meats you wish. Fry in lard. Take white bread, broken up in beef broth, and strain. Boil with your meat. Grate ginger, cinnamon, infuse with verjuice. Boil it all together, and do not let it thicken too much.

White Brewet Of Capons

For white brewet of capons, cook in water and wine. Cut up into parts. Fry in lard, crush almonds. Infuse the crushed almonds with broth. Boil on your meat. Beat ginger, cinnamon and clove, paradise seed, galanga and long pepper. Boil together, and add well beaten egg yolks. This should be quite thick.

Hare Bousac

For bousac of hare or rabbit, brown on the spit or on the grill, then cut up into pieces, and fry in lard. Take browned bread, infuse with beef broth and wine. Strain, mix with verjuice. It should be very black and not too thick.

Houdet Of Capons

For houdet of capons, cook in wine and water, then cut up into pieces. Fry in lard. Take a little burned bread, infuse with your broth and boil with your meat. Powder ginger, cinnamon, clove, paradise seed, and saffron for color.

Civet

For civet, brown on the spit completely raw or on the grill, without letting it cook too long. Then cut up into pieces and brown in lard with onions chopped up small. Then take bread browned on the grill, infuse with wine and beef broth and purée of peas. Boil with your meat. Then powder ginger, cinnamon, clove, paradise seed, and saffron to give color. Infuse it with verjuice and vinegar, and spice it well.

Civet Of Hare

Must be black and made as above. But do not wash the meat at all.

Civet Of Rabbit

Civet of rabbit must be extremely well-cooked, and made like that for hare.

CHAPTER ON ROASTS

Roast Pig

With verjuice. Some put onions on it. In pastry, with verjuice of grain and fine powder.

Roast Veal

Roasted veal is parboiled and larded, and eaten with cameline in pastry, with fine powder and saffron.

Veal's Caul

For veal's caul, also known as breast meat, cut your veal up finely. Cook it. Fry in lard. Crush ginger and saffron, and scramble eggs. Dribble eggs over it while frying.

Roast Mutton

With a little salt, with cinnamon, or verjuice.

Kid And Lamb

Put it in boiling water and take it out quickly. Put on the spit. Eat with cameline.

Goose

Plume a dry goose. Restore it in water. Roast without lard. Eat with garlic or jance.

Roasted Hens

Lard and eat with cameline, or verjuice, in pastry, with powder and cold sage.

Boiled Fresh Wild Boar

Put in boiling water, then roast and baste with a sauce of ginger, cinnamon, clove, paradise seed, and toasted bread, soaked in wine, verjuice, or vinegar. Once it is cooked, boil it all together, and cut up your meat into pieces. Boil so well that it is clear and black.

Fresh Venison

Any fresh venison which is not marinated is eaten with cameline.

Pigeons

Roast pigeons with their heads on, without the feet. Eat with a little salt.

Assorted Small Birds

Pluck while dry. Restore in water. Lard, roast. Eat with salt; also in pastry.

Turtle Doves

Like a goose. If desired, gild along the side and cook with its feet on. Split the head down to the middle of the shoulders, and kill through the heart. Eat with yellow pepper.

Peacock

Also like swan; eaten with a little salt.

[*This document does not include a recipe for swan – this reference is one indication of the manuscript's general incoherence.*]

Storks

Pluck while dry, leaving the feet and the head. Sprinkle and flambé with lard. Eat with a little salt.

Pheasants

Pluck pheasants while dry. Cut off the heads and the tails. When it is roasted, attach the head and the tail to the body with a little wooden dowel. The neck must be upright, and the head must not be cooked.

Bittern, Cormorant

As for the stork and the heron.

Heron

Bleed it and split it up to the shoulders. Either prepare it like the stork or gild if you prefer. Eat with a little salt.

River Ducks

Pluck river ducks while dry and put in a spit. Retain the fat to make the dodine which must be made with lard or verjuice, and onions. Some prefer it in pieces. Once it is cooked, with the dodine, make toasts. Then pour your dodine over your meat and toast.

Stuffed Suckling Pig

Scald it and put in on the spit. Make the stuffing from the drippings of the piglet, and round slices of cooked pig, egg yolks, *guin* cheese [*possibly a cheese made after the harvest, and so supposedly fattier*], peeled and cooked chestnuts, and fine spice powders, all together. Then put it in the piglet's belly, and close up the hole. Baste in vinegar and boiling lard. Eat with yellow pepper.

Stuffed Poultry

Cut their gizzards. Pluck very well and keep the skin whole. Do not restore them in boiling water. Put a pipe between the skin and flesh and blow up the bird between the shoulders. Do not make too large a hole. Leave the wings and the feet with the body and the head. Make a poultry stuffing, handling it as for pork.

To Gild [The Poultry]

Item: To gild it, take egg yolks. Crush up saffron. Dribble it over your poultry the length of the back to the opening. Watch that it does not burn while roasting.

Mock Grenon

Cook livers and poultry gizzards or finely chopped veal in wine and water. Fry in lard. Crush ginger, cinnamon, clove, paradise seed, [infuse with] wine, verjuice or its own juices, and a large quantity of egg yolks. Dribble over your meat, then boil together. Some put in it a little bread and saffron. It must be very thick, of a yellow color, soured with verjuice and with powdered cinnamon on it.

For A Fish Jelly

For fish jelly, take tenches and eels to thicken it, and pike. Cook it in white wine with the appropriate spices, that is: ginger, paradise seed and a little white mustard. Add saffron as necessary to give color to the jelly, as long as there is enough. Strain your broth. When the fish is cooked, strain it through a cloth. Once it is strained, tightly close the dishes for the fish, and put in water or someplace else cool with the broth over it.

Warm Sauce

To make warm sauce, parboil wild boar or for wild boar bellies or beef bellies, roast them on the spit, and put a dripping pan or frying pan underneath. Sprinkle with beef broth, and cut up the meat into pieces, once it is cooked, and put in a pot. Then take bread, and brown it. Add cinnamon, ginger, paradise seed, with more clove than any of the other spices.. Strain all this with the bread, and make the broth clear. It should not be too strong. Boil in a frying pan or a pot. Once it is boiled, salt lightly and add to the meat.

Chicken Shaken With Ginger

Take whole or cut up in sections, as you like. Restore. Once they are restored, set in a pot to brown. Then take white bread, and soak it moderately with poultry livers, then strain. When they are strained, put them in a pot. Dissolve ginger in verjuice and add it to the pot.

Fromanty

To make fromanty, take spelt wheat and cull it very well, and if is not husked, husk it and wash it very well before cooking it. Then cook it in a pot for a long time, and let it sit. Take enough milk for your wheat, so long as you have enough, and add to the wheat, and boil in a pot, stirring well the whole time to keep it from burning. Afterwards, take as many eggs as the pot can fit. Strain the egg yolks, and once they are strained, take the pot with the wheat and the milk off the fire. Take milk and put it with the eggs, and add the eggs together with the wheat and the milk. Stir well. Watch that the milk is not too hot, because it will burn the eggs which will ruin the fromanty, so that it does not come out nicely. Add salt and a great deal of sugar.

Fish Jelly With Meat Scum On It

Cook your fish or meat in wine, verjuice, or vinegar. Some add a little bread. Then add ginger, cinnamon, clove, paradise seed, pepper, galanga, mastic, nutmeg, saffron to give color. Tie it in a white cloth. Boil with your fish or meat, skimming it the whole time. After, as soon as it is time to serve it, when it is cooked, take your broth in a wooden vessel once it has settled. Put your fish or meat on a white tablecloth, and, if it is fish, skin it and add the [skin] peelings to your broth while straining it the last time. See that the broth is clear and clean, and do not wait to strain it until it is cold, because it will not flow. Then put your fish or meat in bowls and reboil your broth, skimming it the whole time. Then serve it on your fish or meat through the cloth, folded over two or three times. Powder your bowls with powder of cinnamon and mastic. Put them in a cold place, and, if it is fish, put in the drippings and soak clove in them. To make jelly, you must stay alert.

Hundred Dishes Of Jelly

To make a hundred dishes of jelly, take twenty five poussins, six young rabbits, four pigs, thirty legs of veal, four [*eight English*] pints of white vinegar, six *sextiers* [*sixteen English pints*] of white wine, six ells of cloth, three quarter pounds of ginger, paradise seed, three quarter pounds of string ginger, six ounces of saffron, five wooden spoons, two large heads of 'earthy' sorrel, twenty earthen pots, six dishes: and drink for the workers.

Lamprey

For lamprey fried with warm sauce, bleed it by the mouth. Remove the tongue. Have it well bled. Put it on a spit. Keep the blood (because it is fatty) and scald it like an eel on a spit. Then grate ginger, cinnamon, paradise seed, nutmeg and a little browned bread soaked in vinegar and the blood. Blend it all together. Boil briefly then put it in your lamprey, whole. The sauce should not be too black.

Cold Sauce

For cold sauce, take poultry and cook in water, then put it on a white tablecloth and let it cool. Powder ginger, cinnamon, clove, and paradise seeds, then crush parsley and bread together to make a gay green. Strain. Some add cooked yolks, mixed with vinegar. Pour on your poultry in sections. For pork, make the cold sauce without eggs.

Mouthfuls of Rice

For mouthfuls of rice, on a meat day, cull, wash in warm water, then wipe your rice by the fire. Take cow's milk, and wheat, add your rice, and boil together on a low fire. Add the fat from beef broth. During Lent, use almond milk, and sugar the bowls.

MEATS AND SOUPS FOR LENT

Beginning Of Fish

Cook in water, at the evening, in oil. Grind almonds, some of your broth, take ginger, some of your milk and mix together. Serve it on your fish, when it is boiled. For the sick, add sugar.

Green Sauce

Take white bread and boil in vinegar. Then cool. The best green [to use to color this sauce] is wheat. If you do not have that, the other is sorrel or *ressise* [*This rare word usually means a restorative dish, but here appears to mean a green.*] Sauce for meat is made the same way, except that one puts in a bit of sage, and strains it through a cloth. If it is too sour, mix in some white wine. Add ginger and pepper, and no other spices.

Civet Of Oysters

For civet of oysters, scald and wash very well. Parboil and fry in oil with onions. Grate ginger, cinnamon, paradise seed and saffron. Take browned bread soaked in purée of peas or boiled water, with wine and verjuice. Boil together with the oysters.

Roast Pike With Chaudumé

Grate ginger, cinnamon, seed, and saffron. Soak browned bread in purée of peas, wine, or verjuice. Boil, and put on your fish.

Flans And Tarts

To make flans and tart at Lent which have the flavor of cheese, take tenches, *lux** and carps and, especially, eggs and milk. Crush, dissolve in white wine, almond oil and a little verjuice. Cook on the fire.

[**This might be a variant of* lus, *which once meant a variety of pike.*]

Flemish Chaudeau

For Flemish chaudeau, boil a little water. Soak egg yolks in white wine. Boil together. Some put in a little verjuice.

Coulis Of Perch

Cook in water and keep the broth. Crush almonds and the perch together, mix with broth in a little wine. Boil it all together. It should be clear.

Blancmange

For capon blancmange for a sick person, cook in water. Crush almonds, and strain with broth. Boil until thick. Put pomegranates over it.

Fresh Water Fish

Lux, pike, dace, barbell, carp, eels, fresh shad. – cook all of these in water and add salt. Eat with green sauce. Salt the shad, eat with garlic.

Lamprey

Small lampreys with the same sauce as lamprey; in pastry and with fine powder.

Cresme

[*Literally, "cream". Could this be a corruption of* bresme *(bream)?]*
Scald it like eel. Eat with green sauce.

Porpoise

For porpoise, either split along the back or put in thin slices in water. Take wine and the liquid of the fish. Powder ginger, cinnamon, paradise seed, pepper and a little saffron. Boil. Do not make it too yellow.

Gurnard And Red Mullets

For gurnards and red mullets, cook in water, or roast on the grill. Split along the back. Eat with cameline.

Mackerel

Roast fresh on the grill. Add a little salt or mustard.

Salmon

Cook fresh salmon in wine and water. Eat with cameline. Salt it with wine. Add as much spring onion as you like.

Salt Water Fish

For brill, sole, ray, turbot, flounder: cook in water, with wine and verjuice.

Cod

Cook in water. Eat with jance. Salt it, with mustard or butter.

Cuttlefish And Cockles

Fry with onions. Add fine powder.

UNBOILED SAUCES

White cameline, green sauce and garlic camelines, white garlic, and green garlic with fresh herring

Cold Sauce

A cold sauce to keep sea fish. Crush bread, parsley and salad burnet, infuse with vinegar. Crush ginger, cinnamon, pepper, galanga, paradise seed, nutmeg, a little saffron, and infuse with verjuice and vinegar and strain. Pour on your fish. Some put salad burnet on it with the whole root.

BOILED SAUCES

Black Pepper

Crush ginger and browned bread. Infuse with vinegar and verjuice. Strain and boil. Some add seed and galanga to it.

Yellow Pepper

Crush up ginger, pepper, saffron, and browned bread. Infuse with vinegar and verjuice. Boil. Some add seed and galanga to it.

Poitevin Sauce

For Poitevin sauce, crush seed and livers. Infuse with wine and verjuice. Boil, with the fat from the roast. Then pour on your roast by the bowlful.

Jance

Crush almonds, then grind up ginger, string ginger and white bread. Infuse with verjuice and wine. Some like it with cow's milk. Boil when you are ready to serve it.

Green Verjuice

Take sorrel with any grain. Infuse with other verjuice. Strain and put a crust of bread in so that it does not turn.

[DRINKS]

[In the original transcription, the following two recipes are mixed in with the menus that follow.]

Clairet

To make one [*two English*] pint[*s*] of clairet, you need a half [*one full English*] pint of honey of wine of crumbs, and be sure to cook it well with wine, and skim it, and an ounce of strained fine powder, if you wish, as for hypocras.

Hypocras

To make one [*two English*] pint[*s*] of hypocras, you need three eighths of an ounce of fine prepared true cinnamon, an eighth of an ounce of string ginger or two if desired, a sixteenth ounce of clove and paradise seed, six ounces of fine sugar; and make a powder of it, and you must color it all with the wine, and the pot under it, and strain it as long as it will flow, and the more it is strained the better, but do not let it get cold.

Spices Used In The Present Viander

Ginger, cinnamon, clove, paradise seed, pepper, mastic, galanga, fine nutmeg, saffron, cinnamon, sugar, anis and powder.

AFTERMATTER/MEALS

[Taillevent, who died in 1395, could not have written the following. However, these exist in the transcription and give some idea of how to assemble the different dishes.]

Of the feast served in the wood by the sea the sixth day of June, 1455 for my lord of Mayne, and my lady of Chasteaubrun

The FIRST

Whites [*bleaks*?] and feathers covered with violets and bouquets, between dishes of other pasties set on the said large pastie, a green dragnet between the two, and whose sides were silver plated and the tops gilded, and, on each one of these a silver plated crenellated barrel, and the top sky blue, and a banner with the arms of my said lord of Mayne, and some with the other arms of my said lady of Villequier and of my said lady of Chasteaubrun; and in these shovelers, cormorants, herons and other live birds, bearing pennants with the said arms, the bouquets and the said feet of the gilded birds; and each large pastie containing a whole kid, a gosling, three capons, six chickens, six pigeons, a young rabbit; a leg of veal chopped finely with two pounds of fat put in the said pastie, and a quarter pound of hard-boiled egg yolks, larded with clove, salted well, with saffron on them; kept in the oven five long hours.

They had in the dish a stuffed chicken, a half loin of veal similarly simmering, all covered with the said German brewet, and over these gilded wafers, pomegranates and sugared almonds as well.

They had in the dish civet of stag and a quarter hare salted overnight, and nails [*cloves*?] of a crane chick [*? alternately, gruel*] in the middle of the dish.

The SECOND

They had in the dish a loin of veal, a whole kid, a pig, two goslings, a small kid or a portion of kid, a dozen chickens, a dozen pigeons, six young rabbits, two herons: two shovelers, two cormorants, a small hare.

"Hedgehogs" with a stuffed fatty capon in each dish [*sic*] and the appropriate jack bristling under the said capons.

With in each dish four chickens, and Duke's powder over it, and there were gilded eggs and other appropriate mixtures.

A suitable support for the said peacocks.

Sturgeon with parsley and cooked vinegar, then ginger on it, leaves of pennyroyal of vine between the skin and these dressed and put notched in a dish, scattered about.

Wild boar made with fried cream.

Darioles and upside-down stars.

Jelly, half-sweet, half-sour, in a dish, white and dark red, marked with the arms said above.

Fried cream. Duke's powder on it, white of fennel, preserved in sugar, silvered.

Larded milk. Sweetened *jonchées* [*a soft cheese*], sweetened white cream, sugared strawberries, preserved plums steamed in rosewater.

The FIFTH

The wreath [*for holding the dishes?*], wine, spices from the storeroom on stags and swans, made of sugar, and pine nuts, marked with the said arms.

Banquet Of My Lord Of Foyes

THE FIRST COURSE

Poussins with sugar, hares or young rabbits with almond cream, cold sauce, vinegar, venison with soup.

SECOND COURSE

Stuffed kid shoulders, sea pullets, young peacocks in full display, quails with sugar.

THIRD COURSE

Cream dolphins, *lasches* [*small shad-like fish* – or lesches – "slices" - *misspelled?*], game hen, pears, fried oranges, jelly, hare pastie.

FRUIT COURSE

White cream, and strawberries, *jonchées* [a soft cheese], and almonds.

Banquet Of My Lord Of La Marche

And Firstly

Vinaigrette, cretonnée of lard, brewet of cinnamon, venison with clove.

SECOND COURSE

Peacocks, swans, herons, young rabbits with spiced sauce, partridges with sugar.

THIRD COURSE

Capons stuffed with cream, pigeon pastie, kids.

FOURTH COURSE

Eagles, pears with hypocras, gilded thin slices [*of bread or meat*?], jelly, watercress.

FIFTH COURSE

White cream, almonds, nuts, hazelnuts, pears, *jonchées.*

Banquet Of My Lord Of Estampes

FOR THE FIRST DISH

Capons with brewet of cinnamon, chickens with herbs, pickle, navews with venison.

SECOND COURSE

The best roast, peacocks with celery, capon pastie, small hares with bramble vinegar, capons with Jean's most,

THIRD COURSE

Partridges with trimolette. Steamed pigeons. Venison pasties. Jelly and slices.

FOURTH COURSE

Four ["oven" – *meaning a pastry*?], fried cream. Pear pastie. Sugared almonds, nuts and raw pears.

Banquet For My Lady

TABLE DISH

Popie, capes [*type of apple*], cherries with sugar or feathers, lemons.

FIRST COURSE

Chimneyed pastie with sugar. Pigeon pastie. Venison with peas. Boiled chickens. Fresh venison with soups.

SECOND COURSE

Roast. Capon pastie. Quail pasties. Venison set separately... or for afterwards.

THIRD COURSE

Pigeons with sugar and vinegar. Tarts with sugar. Trimolettes with sugar. Must. Banquet of marrow.

The FOURTH COURSE

Emblazoned tarts and dolphins. White jelly and other fried cream. Pears with sugar. New almonds.

FOR FIRST

Hams with sugar, capons with tulle, brewet rappé, barded sugared chickens.

SECOND SERVICE

Swans with *santire*. Peacocks. Herons. Venison. *Foynes* shovelers [*a type of duck*].

THIRD SERVICE

Chickens. Pigeons. Young rabbits. Thin slices. Jelly. Baked cream pancake. Thin gilded slices.

Here ends the book of cooking named Tayllevant
which treats of several things pertaining to cooking.

INDEX

BIBLIOGRAPHY

Taillevent. *Le cuisinier Taillevent.* Toulouse : J. de Guerlins, circa 1518-1520

Taillevent. *Le Viandier de Guillaume Tirel dit Tailleven.t* Ed. J. Pichon and G. Vicaire, Paris, 1892.

Le Dictionnaire de L'Académie Françoise, dédié au Roy. Paris: chez Jean-Baptiste Coignard, 1694.

M. D. C. de l'Académie françoise [Thomas Corneille]. *Dictionnaire des Arts et des Sciences.* Paris: chez la veuve Jean-Baptiste Coignard, impr. ordinaire du Roy & de l'Académie françoise : chez Jean-Baptiste Coignard, impr. & libraire ordinaire du Roy & de l'Académie françoise, 1694.

Bourgeois parisien, un. *Le ménagier de Paris, traité de morale et d'économie domestique composé vers 1393.* Publié pour la première fois par la Société des Bibliophiles François. Paris : imp. de Crapelet, 1846.

Cotgrave, Randle. *A Dictionarie of the French and English Languages.* London, 1611. Reprint, George Olms Verlag, Hildesheim-New York, 1970.

Davidson, Alan. *The Penguin Companion to Food.* Penguin Books, 2002.

Franklin, Alfred. *La vie privée d'autrefois: arts et métiers, modes, moeurs, usages des Parisiens, du XIIe au XVIIIe siècle - VI. Les repas. – 1889.* Paris : E. Plon, Nourrit, 1889.

Furetière, Antoine. *Essais d'un dictionnaire universel, contenant généralement tous les mots françois tant vieux que modernes, & les termes de toutes les sciences & des arts.* 1684.

Godefroy, Frédéric. *Dictionnaire de L'Ancienne Langue Française et de Tout Ses Dialectes du IX au XV Siècle.* Paris: F. Vieweg, 1881.

Legrand d'Aussy, Pierre Jean-Baptiste. *Histoire de la vie privée des français, depuis l'origine de la nation jusqu'à nos jours.* Paris : P.-D. Pierres, 1782.

Montagné, Prosper. *Larousse Gastronomique.* New York: Crown Publishers, Inc., 1961.

Web sites:

GLOSSARY OF MEDIEVAL & RENAISSANCE CULINARY TERMS
http://www.thousandeggs.com/glossary.htm

Gernot Katzer's Spice Pages
http://www-ang.kfunigraz.ac.at/~katzer/engl/index.html

CPSIA information can be obtained
at www.ICGtesting.com
Printed in the USA
BVHW041356120922
646808BV00003B/192